Natures Three Daughters by Margaret Cavendish

Beauty, Love & Wit

Part II (of II)

Margaret Lucas Cavendish, Duchess of Newcastle-upon-Tyne was born in 1623 in Colchester, Essex into a family of comfortable means.

As the youngest of eight children she spent much time with her siblings. Margaret had no formal education but she did have access to scholarly libraries and tutors, although she later said the children paid little attention to the tutors, who were there 'rather for formality than benefit'.

From an early age Margaret was already assembling her thoughts for future works despite the then conditions of society that women did not partake in public authorship. For England it was also a time of Civil War. The Royalists were being pushed back and Parliamentary forces were in the ascendancy.

Despite these obvious dangers, when Queen Henrietta Maria was in Oxford, Margaret asked her mother for permission to become one of her Ladies-in-waiting. She was accepted and, in 1644, accompanied the Queen into exile in France. This took her away from her family for the first time.

Despite living at the Court of the young King Louis XIV, life for the young Margaret was not what she expected. She was far from her home and her confidence had been replaced by shyness and difficulties fitting in to the grandeur of her surroundings and the eminence of her company.

Margaret told her mother she wanted to leave the Court. Her mother was adamant that she should stay and not disgrace herself by leaving. She provided additional funds for her to make life easier. Margaret remained. It was now also that she met and married William Cavendish who, at the time, was the Marquis of Newcastle (and later Duke). He was also 30 years her senior and previously married with two children.

As Royalists, a return to life in England was not yet possible. They would remain in exile in Paris, Rotterdam and Antwerp until the restoration of the crown in 1660 although Margaret was able to return for attention to some estate matters.

Along with her husband's brother, Sir Charles Cavendish, she travelled to England after having been told that her husband's estate (taken from him due to his being a royalist) was to be sold and that she, as his wife, would receive some benefit of the sale. She received nothing. She left England to be with her husband again.

The couple were devoted to each other. Margaret wrote that he was the only man she was ever in love with, loving him not for title, wealth or power, but for merit, justice, gratitude, duty, and fidelity. She also relied upon him for support in her career. The marriage provided no children despite efforts made by her physician to overcome her inability to conceive.

Margaret's first book, 'Poems and Fancies', was published in 1653; it was a collection of poems, epistles and prose pieces which explores her philosophical, scientific and aesthetic ideas.

For a woman at this time writing and publishing were avenues they had great difficulty in pursuing. Added to this was Margaret's range of subjects. She wrote across a number of issues including gender, power, manners, scientific method, and philosophy.

She always claimed she had too much time on her hands and was therefore able to indulge her love of writing. As a playwright she produced many works although most are as closet dramas. (This is a play not intended to be performed onstage, but instead read by a solitary reader or perhaps out loud in a small group. For Margaret the rigours of exile, her gender and Cromwell's closing of the theatres mean this was her early vehicle of choice and, despite these handicaps, she became one of the most well-known playwrights in England)

Her utopian romance, 'The Blazing World', (1666) is one of the earliest examples of science fiction. Margaret also published extensively in natural philosophy and early modern science; at least a dozen books.

She was the first woman to attend a meeting at Royal Society of London in 1667 and she criticized and engaged with members and philosophers Thomas Hobbes, René Descartes, and Robert Boyle.

Margaret was always defended against any criticism by her husband and he also contributed to some of her works. She also gives him credit as her writing tutor.

Perhaps a little strangely she said her ambition despite her shyness, was to have everlasting fame. During her career, from the mid 1650's until her death, she was prolific. In recent decades her work has undergone a resurgence of interest propelled mainly by her ground-breaking attitude and accomplishments in those male straitened times.

Margaret Cavendish died on 15th December 1673 and was buried at Westminster Abbey.

Index of Contents

NATURES THREE DAUGHTERS, BEAUTY, LOVE & WIT

PART II

THE ACTORS NAMES
Monsieur Nobilissimo
Monsieur Heroick his Brother
Monsieur Esperance
Monsieur Phantasie
Monsieur Amy
Monsieur Poverty, and other Gentlemen
Madamoiselle Esperance
Madamoiselle La Belle
Madamoiselle Amour
Madamoiselle Grand Esprit
Madamoiselle Bon
Madamoiselle Tell-truth
Madamoiselle Spightfull
Madamoiselle Malicious
Madamoiselle Detractor

ACT I

SCENE I

Enter **MADAMOISELLE GRAND ESPRIT**, and her **AUDIENCE**.

MADAMOISELLE GRAND ESPRIT
Great Fame my Prayers I direct to thee, That thou wilt keep me in thy memory; And place my Name in thy large brazen Tower, That neither Spight, nor Time may it devour; And write it plain, that every age

may see, My Names inscrib'd to live eternally: Let not Malice obstruct my Wit with spight, But let it shine in its own clear light.

Noble and Right Honourable,
I divide my discourse into three parts, as namely Vanity, Vice, and Wickedness; Vanity lives in the Customs and Manners of men, and Wickedness in the Souls of men, Vices in the Senses of men, as vain habits, evill appetites, and wicked passions; as for Vanity and Vice, they are commodities that are sold out of the Shops of Idleness; Vice is sold by wholesale, but Vanities are sold by retail; the Buyers of these Commodities are Youth, the Merchants, are evill Customs, and ill examples; the Masculine youth buyes more Vice than Vanity, and the Effeminate youth buyes more Vanity than Vice; but they all buy, as fast as they can be sold; they will spare for no cost, and will give any prices, although it be their Healths, Lives, Fortunes, or Reputations; as for Wickedness, it is inlayed into the soul like as Mosaickwork, and so close it is wrought therein, as it makes it appear to be the soul it self; but evill Education and Custome, are the Artificers of this work, and not natural Creation, or divine infusion, or inspiration, from whence the Soul proceeds, or is produced, for neither the Gods, nor Nature, is the Author of Wickedness; but Vanity, Vice, and Wickedness, are soon catcht, and like the Plague, they infect all they come near, and Vanity, Vice, and Wickedness is soon learn'd, when Virtue, Goodness, and Piety, are hard Lessons; for though Divines and natural Philosophers, Preaches, and so teaches them, yet they are seldom understood; for if they were, the benefit would be known, and men would pious and virtuous be, for profits sake; for Common-wealths that are composed, and governed by Virtue, Religion, and good Life, they are so strongly united by honest love, as they become inpregnable against Forein Foes, or home factions, or temptations, so live in peace and plenty, which breeds both pleasure and delight; for life doth never truly injoy it self, but in rest, ease, and peace; but to conclude most Noble and Right Honourable, the Soul, Sense, and Education, should be plain with Truth, smooth with Virtue, and bright with Piety, or Zeal; that the Body may live Easily, the life Peaceably, and that the Soul may be blessed with Everlasting Glory.

[Exit.

SCENE II

Enter **MONSIEUR NOBILISSIMO**, and three or four **GENTLEMEN**.

FIRST GENTLEMAN
The Ladies of this Age, are as inconstant as a fevourish pulse, and their affections have more fainting fits, than those are troubled with Epilepses.

SECOND GENTLEMAN
Faith they will hang about ones neck one hour, and spit in his Face the next.

THIRD GENTLEMAN
That is because they would have variety, for they respect Strangers more than friends; for they will entertain Strangers with the civillest Behaviours, fairest Faces, and costliest Garments they have, and make them welcome with their best Cheer, when as their best Friends, lovingest Servants, and oldest Acquaintance, they will neglect, despise, scorn, command, and rail against, and quarrel with.

MONSIEUR NOBILISSIMO

O Gentlemen, brave Cavaliers as you all are, you must never complain, discommend, nor condemn the Actions of the Effeminate Sex; for that we are apt to call their Cruelty, is their Justice, our Sex meriting not their favours; and whensoever we receive the least favours from that Sex, we ought to give thanks, as proceeding from a compassionate Goodness, gentle Nature, sweet Dispositions, and generous Souls, and not as a due, or a debt for our service: for we are bound by Nature, not only to be their Servants, but their Slaves, to be lasht with their frowns, if we be not diligent to their commands, present at their calls, industrious in their service, and our neglects ought to be severely punished; for we wear our lives only for their sakes, as to defend their Honours, to protect their Persons, to obey their Commands, and to please and delight their humours; also the Estates we manage is theirs, not ours, we are but their Stuards, to Husband and increase their Stores, to receive their Revenues, and lay out their Expences, for we have nothing we call our own, since we our selves are theirs; wherefore it is enough for us to admire their Beautyes, to applaud their Wit, to worship their Virtues, and give thanks for their Favours.

[Exeunt.

SCENE III

Enter **MONSIEUR ESPERANCE**, and his Wife **MADAMOISELLE ESPERANCE**.

MONSIEUR ESPERANCE
Wife, why art thou all undrest to day?

MADAMOISELLE ESPERANCE
The truth is, I am become negligent in dressing, since you only esteem my Virtue, not my Habit,

MONSIEUR ESPERANCE
I would have you change into as many several dresses, as Protheus shapes; for it is not the dress can make me Jealous now, for I am confident no Vanity can corrupt thy Virtue, but that thy Virtue can convert Vanity to a pious use or end.

MADAMOISELLE ESPERANCE
Well Husband, I shall study to form my self, and fashion my dress, both to your fancy and desire.

MONSIEUR ESPERANCE
Do so Wife.

[**MONSIEUR ESPERANCE** goes out.

[**MADAMOISELLE ESPERANCE** alone.

MADAMOISELLE ESPERANCE
Ha, is my Husband so confident of me, it is an ill sign from extreme Jealousy, to an extreme Confidence, the next will be a Carelessness, and then a Neglect, and there is nothing my Nature doth more abhor than neglect, for Jealousy proceeds from Love, but Neglect proceeds from a despising, if not a hating; besides, he desires variety of dresses, which shows my Beauty is vaded, or he is weary in viewing of one

object often; but I find his humour is wandring, and seeks for change; if he should prove false, O how unhappy should I be, for I am naturally honest, also my birth and education hath been honest; besides my affections are so fixt as not to be removed: thus I am tyed, and cannot take liberty which other women do, for to divert the sorrows of my heart, or to revenge my wrongs; but I shall mourn, and weep my self to Water, and sigh my self to Ayre.

[Exit.

ACT II

SCENE IV

Enter **MONSIEUR NOBILISSIMO**, and **MADAMOISELLE AMOR**, and **MADAMOISELLE LA BELLE** comes and peeps through the Hangings, and sees them.

MONSIEUR NOBILISSIMO
The bond of our Love is written in large profession, but not sealed with the contracting kiss yet.

[**MONSIEUR NOBILISSIMO** salutes his Mistriss **MADAMOISELLE AMOR**. Her Sister **MADAMOISELLE LA BELLE** comes forth from behind the Hangings.

MADAMOISELLE LA BELLE
So Sister, are not you asham'd?

MADAMOISELLE AMOR
No truly; for my love is so honest, and the subject of my love so worthy, as I am so far from being ashamed to own it, as I glory in my affection.

MADAMOISELLE LA BELLE
I only wonder that with so small acquaintaince, such a familiar friendship should be made.

MADAMOISELLE AMOR
You have no cause to wonder, for Innocency is easily known, tis craft and subtilty that is obscure, and treacherous falshood with leering Eyes, doth at a distance stand, when honesty and truth straight joyns in friendships bonds.

MONSIEUR NOBILISSIMO
My Sweet, Innocent, Virtuous, Wise, Mistriss.

[Kisseth her hand.

[Exeunt.]

SCENE V

Enter **MADAMOISELLE DETRACTOR, MADAMOISELLE SPIGHTFULL, MADAMOISELLE MALICIOUS,** and **MADAMOISELLE TELL-TRUTH**

MADAMOISELLE TELL-TRUTH
I pitty poor Madamoiselle Bon.

MADAMOISELLE SPIGHTFULL
Why so?

MADAMOISELLE TELL-TRUTH
Because she is forsaken.

MADAMOISELLE SPIGHTFULL
I cannot pitty a Fool.

MADAMOISELLE TELL-TRUTH
Why, she is no Fool.

MADAMOISELLE SPIGHTFULL
Yes Faith but she is, to be constant to an unconstant man.

MADAMOISELLE MALICIOUS
The truth is, I think that woman wisest that forsakes before she is forsaken.

MADAMOISELLE TELL-TRUTH
But how and if she meets with a constant man?

MADAMOISELLE DETRACTOR
That she cannot do, for there is no man constant; for they are all false, and more changing than women are.

MADAMOISELLE MALICIOUS
If any should prove unconstant to me, I would Pistoll him.

MADAMOISELLE TELL-TRUTH
Yes with the Gunpowder breath, the Bullets of words, and the Fire of anger, which will do them no hurt.

MADAMOISELLE SPIGHTFULL
The best revenge I know against an Inconstant Man is, to despise him.

MADAMOISELLE TELL-TRUTH
He will not care for your despisements, but Patience, Patience is the best remedy, for then a woman will be content, although she hath not her desires.

MADAMOISELLE MALICIOUS
Can any Creature be content without the fruition of desire?

MADAMOISELLE TELL-TRUTH

Those that cannot, must be unhappy all their Life.

MADAMOISELLE DETRACTOR

Then all Mankind is unhappy, for I dare swear, there is not any that can be content without the fruition of desire; for desire is so restless, as it gives no time for content.

MADAMOISELLE SPIGHTFULL

The truth is, content only lives in words, but never lives in deeds; for I never heard, or saw any one truly content in my life.

MADAMOISELLE TELL-TRUTH

The truth is, Content is like the Shadow of a Substance, or the Thought of an Act, and therefore let us leave it, as we would idle, or vain Thoughts, or vading, or vanishing Shadows.

[Exeunt.

SCENE VI

Enter **MONSIEUR HEROICK**, and **MONSIEUR PHANTASIE**

MONSIEUR PHANTASIE

Sir, it is reported you are a Servant to my Mistriss.

MONSIEUR HEROICK

I am a Servant to the whole Effeminate Sex, and to her, if she be a woman.

MONSIEUR PHANTASIE

Yes, she is a woman, and the fairest of her kind.

MONSIEUR HEROICK

Why then I am her Slave.

MONSIEUR PHANTASIE

I desire you will inslave your self to some other, and not to her.

MONSIEUR HEROICK

You must pardon me if she be the fairest, for I am bound to the absolutest Beauty.

MONSIEUR PHANTASIE

Draw.

MONSIEUR HEROICK

Nay, I am not so rash; for by your favour I will view her with mine own Eyes, and take the opinion of my own Judgment, and not venture my life on your bare word.

MONSIEUR PHANTASIE
I say draw.

MONSIEUR HEROICK
I shall, but know, I only fight in mine own defence, not for her Beauty, unless I saw her, and approved her such as you affirm her to be: for though I am Servant to all, yet tis impossible all should be an absolute Beauty.

MONSIEUR PHANTASIE
Know, I account all those my Enemyes that question it; besides you give me the lye in doubting the truth.

MONSIEUR HEROICK
I perceive it is your violent passion that perswades you, or rather forces you to fight, and not your Reason; and if your passion were to be counselled, I would counsel you to stay, untill we choose our Seconds, to witness how we fought, not in a furious rage, but when our spirits are fresh and cool, our Minds as equal temper'd as our Blades, and that our valours are not ashamed to own the quarrel; so shall we fight on just and honest grounds, and honour will be the purchase we shall gain.

MONSIEUR PHANTASIE
Ile hear no more but fight.

MONSIEUR HEROICK
Nature, I ask thy pardon, I must ingage thee to a furious rage, or sudden fit, or frantick humour, which are for thee to scorn, and slight, and not to fight.

[Exeunt.

SCENE VII

Enter **MONSIEUR NOBILISSIMO**, and **MONSIEUR POVERTY**.

MONSIEUR NOBILISSIMO
Monsieur Poverty, shall I never have the honour of your Company?

MONSIEUR POVERTY
My Poverty will disgrace you my Noble Lord.

MONSIEUR NOBILISSIMO
I were no noble Lord, if virtuous Poverty could disgrace me.

MONSIEUR POVERTY
Howsoever, your Servants, Friends, and Acquaintance will forsake you, if I should wait upon your Lordship.

MONSIEUR NOBILISSIMO

They may be my Acquaintance, but neither my Friends, nor Servants that will forsake me, for the sake of virtuous Poverty: for though I would not have thee intail'd to my line and posterity, nor to live constantly in my family; yet, I am neither ashamed, nor afraid to shake thee by the hand, as long as thou art an honest man; and I desire to take Plenty in own hand, but to serve Poverty with both hands.

MONSIEUR POVERTY
May Plenty be always your Lordships Hand-Maid.

MONSIEUR NOBILISSIMO
And your Reliever Sir.

[Exeunt.

SCENE VIII

[Enter **MADAMOISELLE AMOR**, and her Sister **MADAMOISELLE LA BELLE**.

MADAMOISELLE LA BELLE
Sister, be not jealous of me, for I have no design to rob you of your Servant, I study not those Amorous allurements; for I would not be otherwise known unto the Masculine Sex, than Angels are to one another; yet I may respect honour, and admire without a doteing fondness, or a surprized affection, or an incaptivated love.

MADAMOISELLE AMOR
Yes Sister, when I consider your Virtue, I cannot be Jealous of you, but when I look on your Beauty, I cannot be Confident of my Servant; for Beauty is victorious, and most commonly triumphs in all hearts, binding the Passions, and leading the Affections as Prisoners; and the Thoughts run a-long as Slaves, and Constancy, if it be not kill'd in the Battell, yet it is sore wounded, and if it should recover, yet never to the former strength again.

[Enter **MONSIEUR NOBILISSIMO**.

MADAMOISELLE LA BELLE
My Lord what say you, hath your Mistriss my Sister Amor any reason to be Jealous?

MONSIEUR NOBILISSIMO
Yes, if my Mistriss were any other but her self.

MADAMOISELLE LA BELLE
I thank you; for I had rather be kill'd with civill although dissembling words, than live with rude Inconstancy.

MONSIEUR NOBILISSIMO
Why, do you think I speak not truth?

MADAMOISELLE AMOR

I hope your words are marks of truth, for all belief to shoot at.

MONSIEUR NOBILISSIMO
But Hopes are built on Doubts and Fears, and do you Doubt and Fear my Love?

MADAMOISELLE AMOR
How can I love without attending Fear, being inseparable?

MONSIEUR NOBILISSIMO
Pray do not fear; for though there is none that seeth your Sister La Belle, but must confess she is most beautifull, yet all fancy not Beauty alike; but were she above what she is, as much as Heaven to Earth, or Gods to Men, yet I am fixt, and not to be remov'd, no more than is Eternity.

[Exeunt.

ACT III

SCENE IX

Enter **MADAMOISELLE ESPERANCE** very fine, and her Cousin **MADAMOISELLE TELL-TRUTH**.

MADAMOISELLE ESPERANCE
Am not I very fine to day?

MADAMOISELLE TELL-TRUTH
Yes very fine.

MADAMOISELLE ESPERANCE
Do I look handsome to Day?

MADAMOISELLE TELL-TRUTH
Yes very handsome.

MADAMOISELLE ESPERANCE
If I were a Stranger, should I attract your Eyes to take notice of me?

MADAMOISELLE TELL-TRUTH
As you are my Cousin, and intimate Friend, and known acquaintance, and see you every day, yet I cannot choose but look on you, and take notice of your rich Garments; but why do you ask, for you do not use to make such questions?

MADAMOISELLE ESPERANCE
I will tell you, when I was new Married, my Husband took so much notice of my Dress, that the least alteration he observed; nay he grew jealous at it, and thought each curl a snare set to catch Lovers in; after I had been Married some little space of time, he condemned me for carelessness, and desired me to various dresses; and now drest, or undrest, he never observes; for were I drest with splendrous light,

as glorious as the Sun, or Clouded like dark Night, it were all one to him; neither would strike his Sense; yet I observe he doth observe my Maids, as that one hath a fine Pettycoat, and another hath handsome made Shooes, and then he pulls up their Pettycoats a little way, to see what stockings they have, and so views them all over, and commends them, saying, they are very fine, when all these Garments he commends on them, were mine, which I had cast off, and given to them; when those Garments though fresh and new, when I did wear them, he never took notice of; besides, when my Maids do come into the Room where he and I are, he strives to talk his best, as if he wisht, and did indeavour their good opinion, when only alone with me the rubbish of his discourse doth serve the turn.

MADAMOISELLE TELL-TRUTH
Madam, I perceive you do begin to be Jealous.

MADAMOISELLE ESPERANCE
Have I not reason?

MADAMOISELLE TELL-TRUTH
No truly; for a Man may do such light actions, or speak merrily, or solidly, without an evill design, only to pass a way idle time.

MADAMOISELLE ESPERANCE
Lord how idly you speak Cousin, as to think men might idly pass away their time, when Nature allows life no idle time; for all things are growing, or decaying, feeding life, or getting food for to nourish life, or bearing, or breeding for increase; and man which only by his shape exceeds all other Creatures in Reason, Knowledge, and Understanding, and will you have him cast away these supreme gifts of Nature with idle time? would you have men follow the Sense only, like a Beast, and not to be guided by reason to some noble study, or profitable action? would you have them yield to their surfeting Appetites, and not indeavour to temper them? is Sickness less painfull than Health? is Disorder to be prefer'd before Method, or Inconveniency before Conveniency, Warrs before Peace, Famine before Plenty, Vice before Virtue? all which would be if idle time wery allow'd; for Idleness never found out Arts nor Sciences, or rules of Government, nor the ease of Temperance, nor the profit of Prudence, nor the commands of Fortitude, nor the peace of Justice, which Industry produceth; but Idleness brings Confusion.

[Exeunt.

SCENE X

Enter **MONSIEUR HEROICK** with his Sword bloody, and meets his friend **MONSIEUR AMY**.

MONSIEUR AMY
What hast thou been doing, that thy sword is bloody?

MONSIEUR HEROICK
Fighting.

MONSIEUR AMY
With whom?

MONSIEUR HEROICK
I know not.

MONSIEUR AMY
For what did you fight?

MONSIEUR HEROICK
For nothing, or at least as bad as nothing; for that I never saw, nor heard of, nor knew where to find.

MONSIEUR AMY
This is a strange quarrel, that you neither know the man, nor the cause, it was a mad quarrel.

MONSIEUR HEROICK
You say right; for as for my part I had little reason to fight, I know not what my opposite had: but prithy friend go help him, for he lyes yonder, and I doubt he is deadly wounded, the whilst I will seek a Chirurgion to send to him.

MONSIEUR AMY
You had need seek one for your self, for you bleed I see by your shirt.

MONSIEUR HEROICK
Yes so I will, but it shall be the Lady that was cause of the wounds, and I will try if her Beauty can heal them.

[Exeunt.

SCENE XI

Enter **MONSIEUR NOBILISSIMO**, and **MADAMOISELLE AMOR**.

MONSIEUR NOBILISSIMO
My sweet Mistriss, what is the cause you look so pale and Melancholy?

MADAMOISELLE AMOR
I hear you have forsaken me, and making love to another; which I no sooner heard, but shook with fear, like to a tender Plant blown by a Northern wind, wherewith my blood congeal'd with cold, my thoughts grew sad, and gathered like black Clouds, which makes my head hang down, my face all wither'd pile and dry: but did I love, as many do, for Person, not for Mind, your Inconstancy would be a less Crime; but were your Body as curious made, as Natures skill could form you, and not a Soul answerable, I might Admire you, but not Love you with adoration as I do.

MONSIEUR NOBILISSIMO
Fear not: for as thy Tongue unlocks my Ears, so it locks up my Heart from all thy Sex but thee; and as a Cabinet doth keep thy Picture there.

MADAMOISELLE AMOR

Heaven grant my Tongue may never rust, but move with words, as smoothed with Oyl, turned by the strength of Wit, easy and free.

MONSIEUR NOBILISSIMO

Dear Mistriss banish this Jealousy, it may in time corrupt pure love, and be you confident of my Affection, as of your own Virtue.

MADAMOISELLE AMOR

Your kind words I will take for a sufficient Seal, and never doubt the Bond that Love hath made.

[Exeunt.

SCENE XII

Enter **MONSIEUR PHANTASIE** wounded, being lead between **MADAMOISELLE BON**, and **MONSIEUR AMY**; he seems to be so faint, as not to pass any further, but is forced to ly down, **MADAMOISELLE BON** sits by him.

MONSIEUR AMY

I will go fetch more help and Chirurgions.

[**MONSIEUR AMY** goes out.

[**MADAMOISELLE BON** stayes, and holds her Arm under his head.

MONSIEUR PHANTASIE

I am wounded more with thoughts of Sorrow, than with my opposites Sword, and wish that Death would strike me in thy Arms, that I might breath my last there, offer up my Soul upon the Altar of thy Breast, and yield my life a Sacrifice unto thy Constancy.

MADAMOISELLE BON

May Death exchange, and take my life that is useless to the World, and spare yours, for noble actions to build a fame thereon.

MONSIEUR PHANTASIE

Speak not so.

MADAMOISELLE BON

If my words offend you, my tongue for ever shall be Dumb.

MONSIEUR PHANTASIE

No, it is your Wish offends, and not your Words; for they are Musick to my Ears, or like to drops of Balsom powr'd therein to heal my wounded Soul.

MADAMOISELLE BON

If that my words could cure your wounds that bleed, rather than want, ile speak till all my breath were spent, no life to form words with.

[She weeps.

MONSIEUR PHANTASIE
Why do you weep?

MADAMOISELLE BON
To see you bleed; but if you bleed to Death, I will weep to Death; and as life issues through your Wounds, so shall life issue through my Eyes, and drown it self in floods of tears.

MONSIEUR PHANTASIE
Forbear, let not the Earth drink up those tears, those precious tears the Gods thirst after.

[Enter **MEN** and take him up, and lay him forth.

[Exeunt.

SCENE XIII

Enter **MADAMOISELLE GRAND ESPRIT**, and her **AUDIENCE**

MADAMOISELLE GRAND ESPRIT
Venus thou Goddess fair, for thy Sons sake, Cupid the God of Love, O let me make A Banquet of sweet Wit to entertain This Noble Company, and feast each brain; And let each several Ear feed with delight, Not be disturb'd with foul malicious spight.

Noble and Right Honourable,
I shall take my discourse at this time out of Beauty, the ground of which discourse is Eyes; Eyes are the Beauty of Beauty; for if the Eyes be not good, the Face though ne'r so fair, or otherwise well featur'd, cannot be pleasing; the truth is, Eyes are the most Curious, Ingenious, Delightfull, and Profitable work in Nature; Curious in the Aspect and Splendor; Ingenious in the form and fashion, Delightfull in the Society, and Profitable in their Commerce, Trade, and Traffick, that they have with all the rest of Natures works: for had not Nature made Eyes, all her works had been lost, as being buryed in everlasting darkness; for it is not only Light that shews her works, but Eyes that see her works: wherefore if Nature had not made Eyes she had lost the glory of Admiration and Adoration, which all her Animal Creatures give her, begot, raised, or proceeding from what they see; besides, not only Light the presenter of objects would have been lost, but Life would have been but only a dull Melancholy Motion for want of sight, and for want of sight life would have wanted knowledge, and so would have been ignorant both of its self and Nature; but now life takes delight by the sight, through the Eyes, and is inamor'd with the Beauties it views; and the Eyes do not only delight themselves and life with what they receive, but with what they send forth; for Eyes are not only passages to let Light, Coulours, Forms, and Figures in, but to let Passions, Affections, Opinions out; besides, the Eyes are not only as Navigable Seas, for the Animal Spirits to Traffick on, and Ports to Anchor in; but they are the Gardens of the Soul, wherein the Soul sits and refreshes it self, and Love the Sun of the Soul, sends forth more glorious Rayes than that Sun in the Sky,

and on those objects they do shine, they both comfort and give a nourishing delight; but yet when the light of love doth reflect, the heat doth increase by double lines, and quickness of motion, which causes many times a Distemper of the Thoughts, which turns to a Feavor in the Mind; but to conclude most Noble and Right Honourable, Eyes are the Starrs which appear only in the Animal Globe, to direct the life in its Voyage, not only to places that life knows, but to new discoveryes; and these Animal Starrs do not only guide the Animal life, but have an influence and various effects on the Soul, and are not only to view the Beauties of all the other works of Nature, but are the chiefest Beauties themselves; and if that Reason that is the Educator of the Life, and chief Ruler and Commander of the Soul, did not cross and hinder the influence of these Animal Starrs, they would prove very fatal to many a one: Wherefore Right Honourable, my Application is, that you obey Reason, and pray unto it as to a Deity, that it may divert the Malignant influences, and cause them to point to a Happy Effect. For which my good wishes shall attend you, That the Gods of these Stars may defend you.

[Exeunt.

ACT IV

SCENE XIV

Enter **MONSIEUR NOBILISSIMO**, and **MONSIEUR HEROICK**.

MONSIEUR NOBILISSIMO
Brother, I may bid you welcome home, for I have not seen you these two years; methinks between Brothers as you and I are should never be absence.

MONSIEUR HEROICK
No faith Brother; for we never have good fortune when we are asunder; for since I parted I hear you are to be Marryed, and I must tell you, I am like to be Hanged.

MONSIEUR NOBILISSIMO
Heaven forbid you should be hanged.

MONSIEUR HEROICK
And do not you make the same Prayer against your Marriage?

MONSIEUR NOBILISSIMO
No, for that prayer would prove a Curse, if Heaven should grant it; but I hope Brother you speak of this but merrily, and not as a truth to believed that you are like to be hanged.

MONSIEUR HEROICK
Yes faith, I met with a man that was resolv'd to fight with the next he met, I think, for he forced a quarrel, and we fought, and I fear I have killed him.

MONSIEUR NOBILISSIMO
What was the cause of the quarrel?

MONSIEUR HEROICK
Why about a Beauty, that none must admire but himself, and yet they must maintain she is the absolutest Beauty of her Sex, and such a Beauty, I hear of every where, but I cannot see her any where.

MONSIEUR NOBILISSIMO
Let me tell you Brother she is worth the seeing.

MONSIEUR HEROICK
And is she worth the blood and life that is lost and spilt for her?

MONSIEUR NOBILISSIMO
Yes, if it had been to maintain her Beauty against rude Despisers, or her Virtue against base Detractors, or her Honour against wicked Violators; for her Soul hath as many beautifull graces and Virtues, and her mind as many noble qualities, as her body hath beautifull Parts, Lineaments, gracefull Motions, pleasing Countenances, lovely Behaviour, and courteous Demeanors.

MONSIEUR HEROICK
Certainly Brother you are very well acquainted with her, that you know her so well, as to speak so confident of her.

MONSIEUR NOBILISSIMO
Yes Brother, I do know her very well, for she is Sister to my Mistriss.

MONSIEUR HEROICK
So, I thought she had some relation to you, that you spake so much in her praise; this Self-love bribes all our Tongues; but Brother, you have so fired my Spirits, as I am almost as mad as the Gentleman I fought with, before I see her, meerly with the report, and since I must lose my Wits with the rest of Mankind, for I find all are mad that come within the list of her Name, pray let me part with my Wits on Honourable terms, as at the view of her Beauty.

MONSIEUR NOBILISSIMO
I shall make it a request to her that you may see her, and she being a person who is very obliging, I make no question but she will receive your civil and humble respects.

[Exeunt.

SCENE XV

Enter **MONSIEUR ESPERANCE**, and his Wife **MADAMOISELLE ESPERANCE**

MADAMOISELLE ESPERANCE
Husband do you love me?

MONSIEUR ESPERANCE
Yes.

MADAMOISELLE ESPERANCE
Better than any other Woman?

MONSIEUR ESPERANCE
I can make no comparison.

MADAMOISELLE ESPERANCE
Why do you then neglect me so much, as to take no notice whether I be fine and brave, or ragged, or patcht, or ilfavoured, or handsom, and yet you take notice of every other woman, from the stranger abroad, to the Kitchin-Maid at home?

MONSIEUR ESPERANCE
By my troth Wife I do so just as I would do of a Tree, or a Bush, or a Stone, or a Brake, or a Fox, or an Ass, and no otherwise.

MADAMOISELLE ESPERANCE
Yet it is a sign you have them in your mind, and I had rather be hated than forgotten; wherefore pray let me be sometimes in your thoughts, although as a Bryar, and not to be flung out Root and Branch.

MONSIEUR ESPERANCE
Heaven forbid Wife you should become a Thorn in my Mind, but thou art there as my Soul, nor do I love you at a common rate: for were thy person more deformed than ever Nature made, either by Sickness or Casualty, I still should love thee for thy Virtuous Soul; and though your person is very handsom, yet I consider not your Beauty but your Health, so you be well, I care not how you look; for my love is at that height as it is beyond the body grown; for should I only love you for your Beauty, when that is decayed, my love must of necessity dy, if Beauty were the life.

MADAMOISELLE ESPERANCE
So then I am only your spiritual love, and you will chuse a temporal one elsewhere.

MONSIEUR ESPERANCE
Prethee be not Jealous of me, because I am become assured of your Chastity; for know, I could sooner hate my self, than love, or amorously affect any other woman but thy self; and when I prove false to you, may Jupiter cast me to Plutoes Court, there to be tormented Eternally.

MADAMOISELLE ESPERANCE
Well, pardon this fit of Jealousy, for I shall never question your affection more, nor doubt your Constancy.

[Exeunt.

SCENE XVI

Enter **MADAMOISELLE LA BELLE**, and her Sister **MADAMOISELLE AMOR**.

MADAMOISELLE LA BELLE

To quarrel and fight for me is strange, for as for the one I never saw, and the other I have no acquaintance with; but had I favoured the one, or affronted the other, or had favoured them both, it might have raised a dispute, from a dispute to a quarrel, from a quarrel to a duell; but many times men make a seeming love the occasion to shew their courage, to get a fame; but what fame soever men get, the woman loses, as being thought either too kind, or cruell.

MADAMOISELLE AMOR
Sister, this Gentleman never saw you, only fought in his own defence; he desires you would give him leave to come and kiss your hands, he is a very gallant man, and an experienced Souldier.

MADAMOISELLE LA BELLE
A Souldier? why he never lead an Army, nor pitcht a Field, nor fought a Battel; he never Intrencht, nor Incampt; he never guarded, kept, nor took Fort, Town, or City; perchance he hath studied as most Gentlemen do, so much of Fortification, as to talk of Trenches, Lines, Ramparts, Bullworks, Curtains, Wings, Faces, Forts, Centries; And of Amunition, Cannon, Muskets, Carabines, Pistols, Slings, Bowes, Arrows, Darts, Pikes, Bills, Halbards, Bolts, Poleaxes, Swords, Cimeters, Shot, Bullets, Powder, Drums, Trumpets, Waggons, Tents and the like; and for Arms, Pot, Back, Breast, Gantlets, Corselets, Gorgets and the like, thus they learn the Names, but seldome practise the use.

MADAMOISELLE AMOR
Yes, this Gentleman hath lead Armies, pitcht Fields, fought Battels, where those he won were won by his Prudence and Conduct, and those he lost were by Fortunes spight, whose changing power, and inconstant humour, no Mortal can withstand.

MADAMOISELLE LA BELLE
Nay Sister, if he be so gallant a person, I shall not refuse his visits, nor deny my self his Company, but entertain him as civilly as he may deserve.

[Exeunt.

ACT V

SCENE XVII

Enter **TWO GENTLEMEN**

FIRST GENTLEMAN
Well met, I was going to your Lodging.

SECOND GENTLEMAN
Faith if you had gone to my Lodging you had mist of my Company.

FIRST GENTLEMAN
But howsoever, I should have been entertained by thy old Landlady, for she makes me welcome in thy absence.

SECOND GENTLEMAN
The truth of it is, that my Landlady as old as she is, loves the Company of men, especially of young men; for if a young man will trouble himself to stay in her Company, and talk to her, she is so pleased, as she makes more wrinckles with her smiles, than Time hath made, and she will simperingly put in her Chin, as if she were but fifteen.

FIRST GENTLEMAN
Faith I commend women, for they will never yield to ages humours, though they are forced to yield to ages infirmities; for their minds are always young, though their bodyes be old.

SECOND GENTLEMAN
Indeed their minds are Girls all their life time; but leaving old women, will you go see Monsieur Phantasie?

FIRST GENTLEMAN
Is he so well as to admit of Visiters?

SECOND GENTLEMAN
Yes, for he is in a recovering condition, and state of Health.

FIRST GENTLEMAN
Come let us go then.

[Exeunt.

SCENE XVIII

Enter **MONSIEUR HEROICK**, and **MADAMOISELLE LA BELLE**

MONSIEUR HEROICK
Madam, the fame of your Beauty and Virtue hath drawn me hither, to offer my service on the altar of your commands.

MADAMOISELLE LA BELLE
You are so great a favourite to Nature and Fortune, and are so splenderous with their gifts, as you are able to put the confidence of our Sex out of Countenance, especially I, that am by Nature bashfull; wherefore it is unlikely I should command you.

MONSIEUR HEROICK
I had rather be commanded by you Lady, than to command the whole World, and should be prouder to be your Slave, than to be that sole Monarch.

MADAMOISELLE LA BELLE
I should be sorry so gallant a man as fame reports you to be; should have so sick a Judgment, and so ungoverned a Passion, as to yield up your liberty to a woman, and to ty your life to her vain foolish humours.

MONSIEUR HEROICK
It is impossible that in so heavenly a form, a foolish Soul should be; for I perceive by your beautifull person; Nature hath outwrought her self, having not Art or skill to make a Second, and what man would not be proud to serve the only she?

MADAMOISELLE LA BELLE
O Sir, take heed you wrong not your noble worth and merit, in being over civill; for complements are all dissembling, and dissembling runs in the ways of perjury.

MONSIEUR HEROICK
Pray Madam conster not my love-service and admiration to an idle Visit, a vain Discourse, and false Profession; for if you appear not so beautifull to all the World, as you appear to me, yet I dare boldly tell the world, I think you so, and will maintain it with my life.

MADAMOISELLE LA BELLE
I believe then I am more beholding to your Eyes that have contracted me into a beautifull form, than unto Nature that hath made me of a vulgar shape.

MONSIEUR HEROICK
Your Tongue Lady hath the power of Circes wand, to charm the Senses, and transform the shape, making all men it speaks to, either to appear Monsters or Gods.

MADAMOISELLE LA BELLE
You have Inthroned me with your Favours, and Crowned me with your Commendations.

MONSIEUR HEROICK
My desire is, that you will Crown me with your Love.

[Exeunt.

SCENE XIX

Enter **MADAMOISELLE DETRACTOR**, **MADAMOISELLE MALICIOUS**, and **MADAMOISELLE TELL-TRUTH**

MADAMOISELLE TELL-TRUTH
I hear that Madamoiselle Bon shall marry her unconstant Servant, Monsieur Phantasie.

MADAMOISELLE DETRACTOR
Faith that is a comfort, that any woman can get a Husband, whilst the Graces are young and in being.

MADAMOISELLE TELL-TRUTH
The Graces never grow old.

MADAMOISELLE DETRACTOR
Let me tell you, Time decays and withers all things.

MADAMOISELLE TELL-TRUTH
No, not the Gods.

MADAMOISELLE DETRACTOR
But Time doth waste Devotion, wears out Religion, burns up the Sacrifice of Praise, puts out the Lamp of Charity, and quenches out the Vestal fire of Zeal.

MADAMOISELLE MALICIOUS
But then there are new Religions brought in the place or room of the old

MADAMOISELLE DETRACTOR
Yes, and new Gods with new Religions, and new Religions and Opinions are like young beautifull Ladyes when they appear first to the view of the World; they are followed, admired, worshiped, sought, sued, and prayed to; but when they grow old, all their Servants and followers forsake them, and seek out those that are younger: so the last and newest Opinions and Religions, are accounted the best, and stuck to for a time the closest, and followed by the greatest numbers, and have most zealous supplicants; thus the Gods dy in effect.

MADAMOISELLE TELL-TRUTH
The truth is, that all things that are young, are Strong, Vigorous, Active and Flourishing; and whatsoever is old, is VVeak, Faint, Sick, and witheringly dyes.

[Enter **MADAMOISELLE SPIGHTFULL**.

MADAMOISELLE SPIGHTFULL
I can tell you news.

MADAMOISELLE TELL-TRUTH
What news?

MADAMOISELLE SPIGHTFULL
Why Monsieur Nobilissimo to is marry Madamoiselle Amor, and his Brother Monsieur Heroick is to marry her Sister Madamoiselle La Belle.

MADAMOISELLE TELL-TRUTH
And who is to marry the third Sister Madamoiselle Grand Esprit.

MADAMOISELLE SPIGHTFULL
She is resolved to live a single life.

MADAMOISELLE DETRACTOR
I am glad they have chose Husbands out of the numbers of there Suters; for when they are married, I hope out of the number of there remainders, we may have some offers for Husbands.

MADAMOISELLE MALICIOUS
For my part I shall despair, unless the third Sister Madamoiselle Grand Esprit would marry also; for the whole bulk of Mankind will sue to her, and never think of any other woman, whilst she is undisposed of.

MADAMOISELLE TELL-TRUTH
But she it seems hath declared she will never marry.

MADAMOISELLE MALICIOUS
That is all one, for men will persue their desires, and live of Hopes so long, as there is any left.

MADAMOISELLE SPIGHTFULL
Well, the worst come to the worst, we shall only live old Maids.

MADAMOISELLE TELL-TRUTH
But not old Virgins.

[Exeunt.

SCENE XX

Enter **MADAMOISELLE GRAND ESPRIT**, her two Sisters **MADAMOISELLE AMOR**, and **MADAMOISELLE LA BELLE** as Brides, and **MONSIEUR NOBILISSIMO**, and **MONSIEUR HEROICK** his Brother, as Bridegrooms, and a Company of **BRIDAL GUESTS** all as her **AUDIENCE**.

MADAMOISELLE GRAND ESPRIT
Great Hymen, I do now petition thee, To bless my Sisters, not to favour me; Unless I were thy subject to obey, But I am Diana's and to her do pray; But give me leave for to decide the cause, And for to speak the truth of marriage laws; Or else through ignorance each man and wife, May rebels prove by Matrimonial strife.

Noble and Right Honourable,
From the root of Self-love grows many several Branches; as Divine Love, Moral Love, Natural and Sympathetical Love, Neighbourly and Matrimonial Love; Divine Love is the Love to the Gods, Moral Love is the Love to Virtue, Natural Love is the Love to Parents and Children, Sympathetical Love is of Lovers, or Friendships, Neighbourly Love is the Love of Acquaintance, and true Matrimonial Love is the Love of United Souls, and Bodyes; but I shall only insist or discourse at this time for my Sisters sakes, of Matrimonial Love; this Matrimonial Love, is the first imbodyed Love that Nature created; for as for Divine Love, and Moral Love, they are as incorporeal as the Soul, and Sympathetical and Matrimonial Love, which I will joyn as Soul and Body, were before Natural, or Neighbourly Love; for Marriage beget; Acquaintance, and none lives so neer nor converses so much as man and wife; and there was a Sympathy and Conjunction of each Sex, before there were Children, and there could be no Parents before there were Children; thus Matrimonial Love was the first substantial Love, and being the Original and producing Love, ought to be honoured and preferr'd as the most perfect and greatest Love in Nature; but mistake me not Noble and Right Honourable, when I say the greatest Love in Nature, I mean not the Supernatural Love, as Divine Love as to the Gods; but this Matrimonial Love, I say is to be the most respected, as the Original Love, like as Nature is to be honoured and preferred before the Creatures she makes; so Matrimonial Love ought to be respected first, as being the cause of Friendly, Sociable, Neighbourly, and Fatherly Love; wherefore man and wife ought to forsake all the world, in respect of each other, and to prefer no other delight before each others good or content; for the Love of

Parents and Children, or any other Love proceeding from Nature, ought to be waved when as they come in Competition with the Love man and wife; for though Matrimonial Love is not such a Divine Love as from man to the Gods, yet it is as the Love of Soul and Body, also it is as a Divine Society, as being a Union; but Right Honourable, to tell you, my opinion is, that I belive very few are truly married; for it is not altogether the Ceremony of the Church nor State that makes a true marriage; but a Union and indissoluble Conjunction of Souls and Bodyes of each Sex; wherefore all those that are allowed of as man and wife, by the Church, State, and Laws, yet they are but Adulterers, unless their Souls, Bodyes, and Affections, are united as one; for its not the joyning of hands, speaking such words by Authentical persons, nor making of vows; and having Witnesses thereof, that makes a true marriage, no more than an Absolution without a Contrition makes a holy man: wherefore dear Sisters, and you two Heroick Worthies, marry as you ought to do, or else live single lives, otherwise your Children will be of a Bastard kind, and your associating but as Beasts, which are worse than Birds, for they orderly chuse their Mates, and lovingly fly and live together, and equally labour to build their nest, to feed their young, and Sympathetically live, and love each other, which order and love few married persons observe, nor practise; but after all this, even those marriages that are the perfectest, purest, lovingest, and most equallest, and Sympathetically joyned, yet at the best marriage is but the womb of trouble, which cannot be avoided, also marriage is the grave or tomb of Wit; for which I am resolved for my part to live a single life, associating my self with my own Thoughts, marrying my self to my own Contemplations, which I hope to conceive and bring forth a Child of Fame, that may live to posterity, and to keep a-live my Memory; not that I condemn those that marry, for I do worship married persons, as accounting them Saints, as being Martyrs for the good cause of the Common-wealth, Sacrificing their own Happiness and Tranquillity, for the weal publick; for there is none that marries that doth not increase their Cares and Pains; but marriage Unites into Familyes, Familyes into Villages, Villages into Cities, Cities into Corporations, Corporations into Common-wealths; this increase keeps up the race of Mankind, and causes Commerce, Trade, and Traffick, all which associates men into an Agreement, and by an Agreement men are bound to Laws, by Laws they are bound to Punishments, by Punishments to Magistrates, and by Magistrates and Punishments to Obedience, by Obedience to Peace and Defence, in which Center of Peace my dear Sisters, I wish you may live, and be guarded with the Circumference of Defence, that nothing may disturb or indanger you or yours; and that you may live in true marriage, and increase with united love, blest with Virtuous Children, and inrich'd with prudent Care, and Industry: also I wish and pray that Jealousy may be banished from your Thoughts, Pains and Sickness from your Bodyes, Poverty from your Familyes, evill Servants from your Imployments, Disobedience from your Children. And that Death may not rob you of your breed, But after your life your Children may succeed.

MARGARET CAVENDISH – A CONCISE BIBLIOGRAPHY

Philosophical Fancies (1653)
Poems and Fancies (1653)
Philosophical and Physical Opinions (1655)
Nature's Pictures drawn by Fancie's Pencil to the Life (1656)
The World's Olio (1655)
Playes, (1662) folio, containing twenty-one plays including
Loves Adventures
The Several Wits
Youths Glory, and Deaths Banquet
The Lady Contemplation

Wits Cabal

The Unnatural Tragedy

The Public Wooing

The Matrimonial Trouble

Nature's Three Daughters (Beauty, Love and Wit) Part I & Part II

The Religious

The Comical Hash

Bell in Campo

A Comedy of the Apocryphal Ladies

The Female Academy

Plays never before printed (1668), containing five plays.

The Sociable Companions, or the Female Wits

The Presence

The Bridals

The Convent of Pleasure

A Piece of a Play

Orations of Divers Sorts (1662)

Philosophical Letters, or Modest Reflections upon some Opinions in Natural Philosophy maintained by several learned authors of the age (1664)

CCXI Sociable Letters (1664)

Observations upon Experimental Philosophy & Description of a New World (1666)

The Blazing World (1666)

The Life of William Cavendish, Duke, Marquis, and Earl of Newcastle, Earl of Ogle, Viscount Mansfield, and Baron of Bolsover, of Ogle, Bothal, and Hepple, &c. (1667)

Grounds of Natural Philosophy (1668)

www.ingramcontent.com/pod-product-compliance
Lightning Source LLC
Chambersburg PA
CBHW021950040426
42448CB00008B/1331